Handmad

Silk Paint Greetings Curas

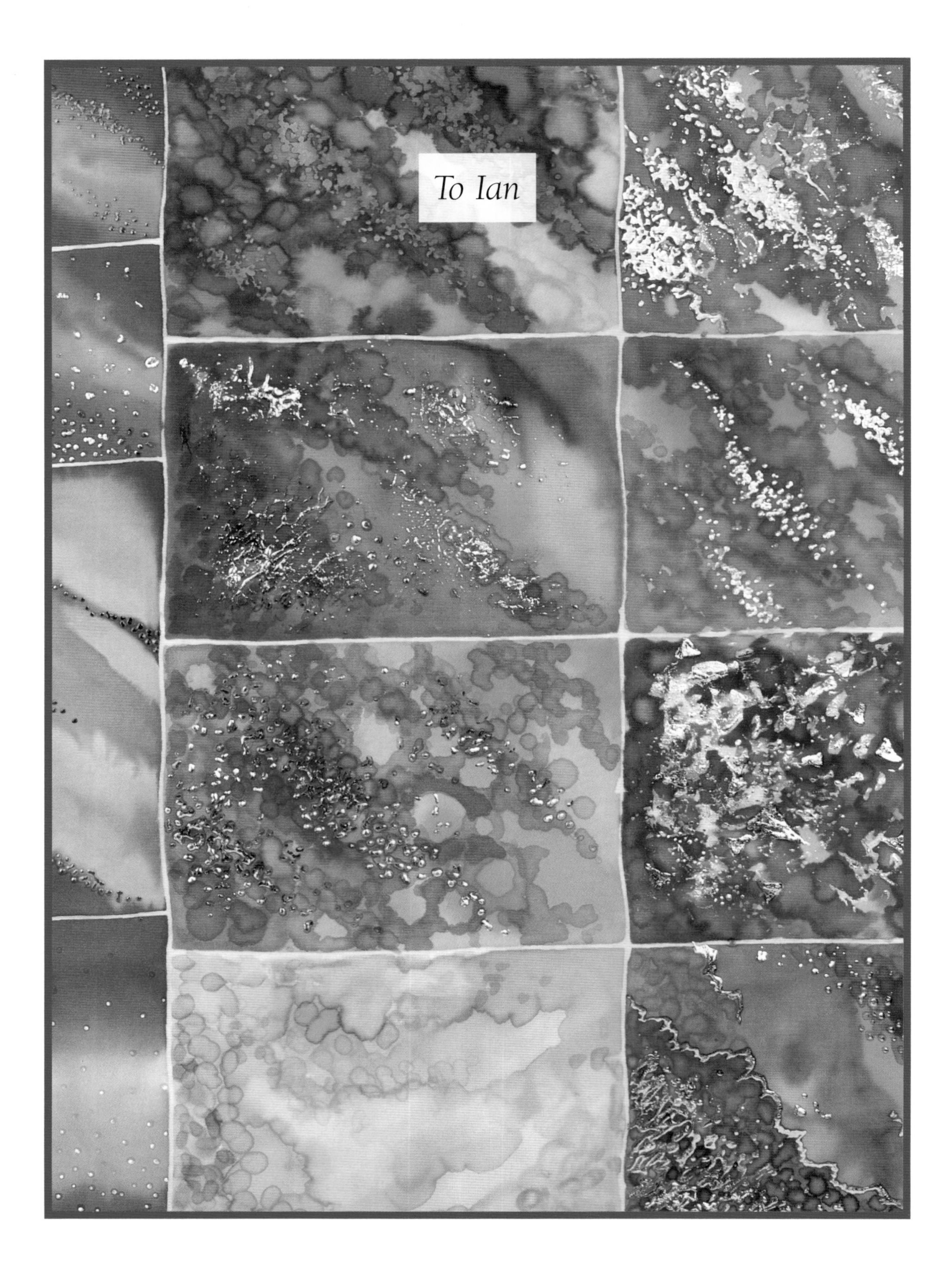

To Ian

Handmade

Silk Painted Greetings Cards

Mandy Southan

SEARCH PRESS

First published in Great Britain 2003

Search Press Limited
Wellwood, North Farm Road,
Tunbridge Wells, Kent TN2 3DR

ISBN 1 903975 80 8

If you have difficulty obtaining any of the equipment or materials mentioned in this book, please visit our website at **www.searchpress.com.**

Alternatively, you can write to the Publishers, at the address above, for a current list of stockists, including firms which operate a mail-order service.

Publishers' note

All the step-by-step photographs in this book feature the author, Mandy Southan, demonstrating how to make handmade greetings cards. No models have been used.

Printed in Spain by Elkar S. Coop., Bilbao 48012

It is always a pleasure working with the team at Search Press and I would like to thank everyone involved in the production of this book, especially Commissioning Editor Roz Dace, Editor Alison Howard and Designer Juan Hayward, and also Roddy Paine for his excellent photography. My thanks also to Craft Creations Ltd. for supplying the greetings card blanks used in this book and to Caroline Munns of Rainbow Silks for sending me lots of materials and exciting new products to help me develop the projects. I am only sorry that there was not enough space to include them all!

Cover
Magic Carpet: *a variation of the project shown on page 30.*

Page 1
Bright Angles: *a variation of the project shown on page 18.*

Page 2
Painted cards: *if you have a lot of cards to make, it saves time if you paint a variety of designs on one large piece of silk.*

Page 3
Peony: a variation *of the project shown on page 24.*

Page 5
All That Glitters: *a variation of the project shown on page 36.*

Contents

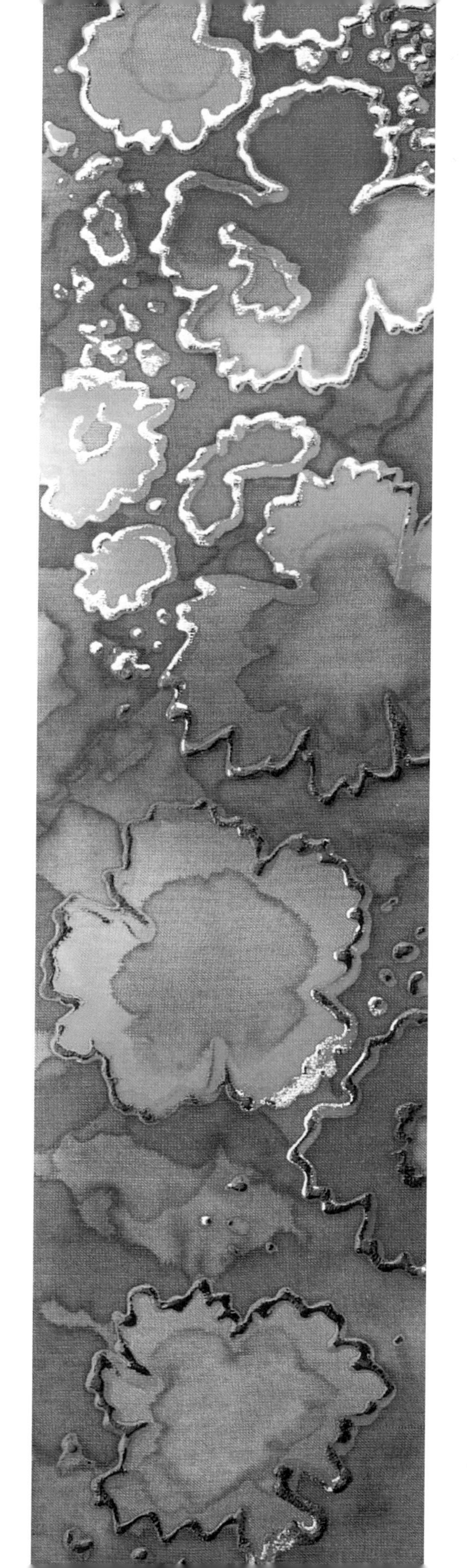

Introduction

Silk painting is a wonderful medium for both large- and small-scale work, and lends itself perfectly to greetings cards. Painted silk cards are easy and fun to make, and the jewel-like colours and luxurious sheen of the fabric make them look very special and eye-catching.

If you have never done any silk painting before you will be surprised how fascinating it is, and greetings cards are ideal first projects. You will not need a lot of expensive equipment, and cards are small enough to complete very quickly. The projects in this book will introduce you to basic silk painting techniques and materials, with designs which you can copy or adapt. It is lovely to design your own cards for special friends, but do not worry if you cannot draw: you can trace from books or magazines, use your own photographs, or just make up abstract patterns like some of the ones featured in this book.

If you have some experience of silk painting, you will find that painting cards gives you an excellent opportunity to enjoy yourself playing with new materials and trying out different designs and colour combinations. There are lots of new and exciting products which can add an extra dimension to your designs – try adding texture and shimmer with glitter liners, metallic paints and foils. There are endless ways of combining new materials with traditional silk painting techniques: in terms of possibilities, each project featured is only the tip of the iceberg!

The projects show different methods for painting and mounting the silk: you can cut your own card mounts or buy them ready cut and simply stick your painted silk to them. Individual cards can be painted on a small embroidery frame or even an old picture frame. If you have a larger silk painting frame, you can divide the silk into sections with gutta and paint quite a few at the same time, as in the panel shown on page 2.

All the projects in this book were painted with colours mixed from the six basic hues shown on page 8. The materials list tells you which were used for each project. Colour mixing takes practice; experiment by making up your own colourways and above all, enjoy the beautiful colours that will appear as if by magic as the paints spread and blend on the silk. I think you will gain as much pleasure from painting silk greetings cards as your friends and family will from receiving them.

Mandy Southan

Opposite: a selection of handmade cards based on the projects in this book.

Materials

Painting the silk

Special paints and dyes are used for silk painting. They spread freely on the silk and do not spoil its sheen. The colours are fixed after painting to make them permanent. Silk painting materials are available from good art and craft shops and also by mail order.

Iron-fix paints

These are ironed to fix the paint. Use a cotton cloth to protect your ironing board and a hot, dry iron on the reverse of the silk so it does not stick to the gutta or outliner. For greetings cards, heating the painted silk with a hot hair dryer should be sufficient to fix the paint.

Steam-fix dyes

Some people are reluctant to use dyes because they think fixing them will be difficult, but it is actually very easy, especially when you are making small pieces for cards. They produce really glowing colours so it is well worth the trouble. Follow the instructions for fixing opposite, and remember the silk must come into contact only with steam, not water. An ice cube tray makes an excellent palette for dyes.

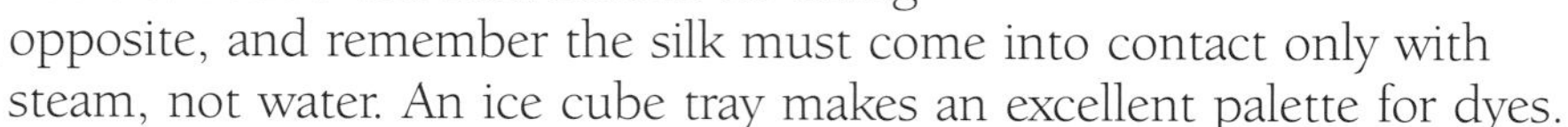

Mixing colours

You only need a few basic colours: choose two reds, two yellows and two blues from either an iron-fix or a steam-fix range – see strip below for guidance. From these you can mix greens, oranges and violets and a wide range of neutral tones. Use a clean brush and palette, and blend the colours into each other on the silk to create further shades. You can dilute colours to make tints using water. Dyes are best diluted with diffusing medium – sometimes called *diluent* or *thinners* – which helps the colours spread evenly.

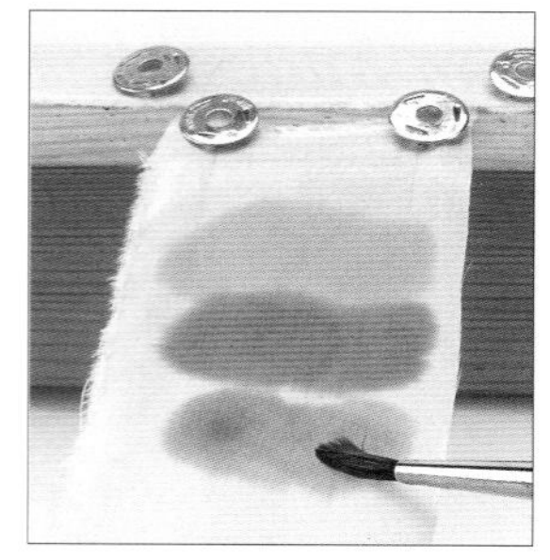

Test the colours you have mixed on a strip of silk

magenta *red* *golden yellow* *lemon yellow* *cyan* *ultramarine*

Fixing silk paints and dyes

Although painted silk used for cards will not be washed, fixing is still advisable. Water droplets can mark unfinished silk, and the card might be delivered by post on a rainy day. Unfixed cards can fade, and your friends may like your cards so much they may want to frame them.

There are two methods of fixing: iron-fix paints are ironed to bond the colours to the silk, while steam-fix dyes become permanent when the painted silk is exposed to hot steam. The steam penetrates the silk and softens the fibres so the dyes bond, without washing away the painted design. Steam fixing enhances the colour of the dyes and restores the sheen of the silk.

You can also fix dyes using a pressure cooker, but not one you use for food. Use absorbent paper and foil as in the method below, and place the roll of silk on a trivet well above the water level. Make sure it does not touch the sides of the pan, or condensation may spoil it. Steaming in the pressure cooker only needs 10 minutes.

After steaming, unroll the silk and iron it to remove any creases. For stubborn creases, or if the paper has stuck to the outlines, rinse it under cold running water, squeeze dry in a towel, and iron while damp.

Note

All equipment and paper used for steaming must be dry so water does not come in contact with the unfixed silk.

Bring the water to the boil before putting the silk on to steam. If the water level needs to be topped up during the process, use boiling water so it does not reduce the temperature of the steam.

Warning: Do not try to fix your work using a steam iron. It is not sufficient, and the water droplets produced will mark the silk.

Steam-fixing

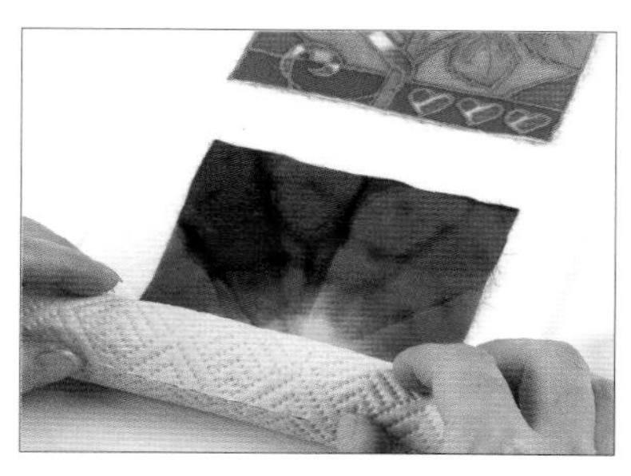

1. Roll the finished paintings in absorbent paper trimmed to just wider than the silk.

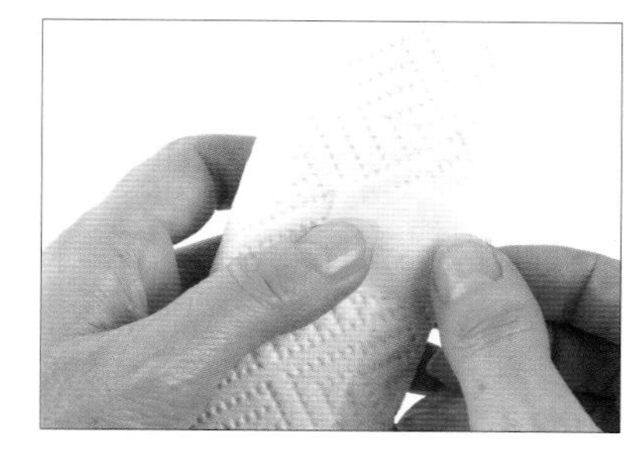

2. Secure the roll with a piece of masking tape.

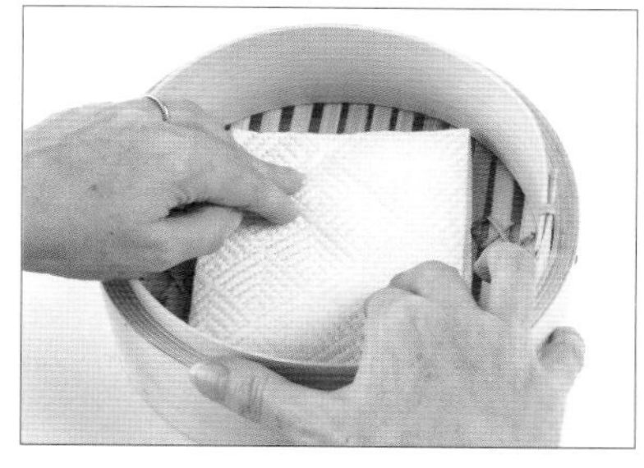

3. Line a steamer – bamboo is best – with absorbent paper. Place the roll on top.

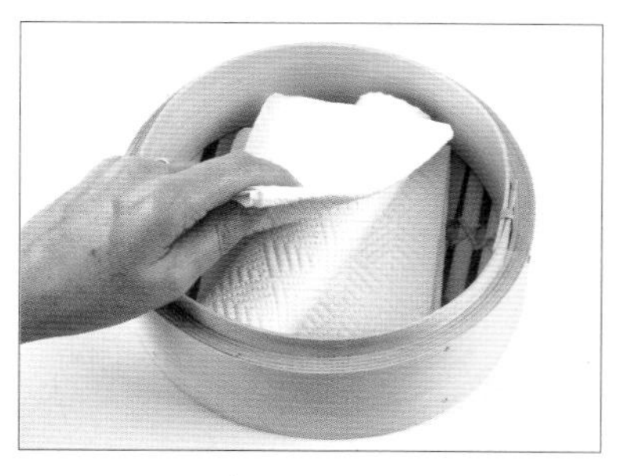

4. Cover the roll of paintings with another paper pad.

5. Cover everything with a circle of aluminium foil.

6. Steam for about an hour over a suitably-sized pan.

Silk painting equipment

You can paint on lots of different types of silk, but **Habotai No. 8** is a useful, multi-purpose silk that is ideal for cards. It is inexpensive, handles and takes paint well, and is thick enough to take a spray adhesive. Using a **wooden frame** prevents the silk touching the work surface when outlining or painting, so the colours can spread evenly and are contained by the resist lines. Adjustable silk painting frames are available in different sizes, or improvise with an old photograph or picture frame. Silk for cards can also be painted on an embroidery frame. You can use **jam jars** for water. **Droppers** are useful for transferring colours or diffusing medium from bottle to palette, or adding water to dilute them. To wash them, fill with water, shake and squirt out until they are clean. **Resist** or **outliner** blocks the silk fibres, preventing colours spreading to adjoining areas. It is usually applied in unbroken lines so colours are contained or separated from each other. Coloured, metallic and pearlised outliner comes in jars or tubes. Water- or spirit-based **gutta** is a clear resist which does not colour the silk. Always empty spirit-based gutta back into the jar after use, or it will thicken in the bottle. Clean the nib with white spirit. Gutta is often applied using a **gutta bottle** fitted with a metal nib, which gives a finer line than a plastic nozzle. **Glitter pens** and **glitter paint** often work as resist too. Attach silk to your frame with three-point **silk pins** which are sharp, easy to push in and will not snag the fabric. Use a round watercolour brush (No. 8) for larger areas of wash and a No. 6 with a good point for the rest. Mix colours in a **palette** or individual dishes and dilute with water or **diffusing medium** (not shown) which helps colours paint on more evenly.

Other equipment

Protect your work surface with **scrap paper** or **polythene sheet** and your clothes with an **apron**. Mount the painted silk on the cards with **spray adhesive,** which is often sold for mounting photographs. It does not soak through and mark the silk, and can be peeled back and repositioned if necessary. You will need an **iron** to remove creases from your work and for iron-fix paints. **Absorbent paper** is useful for mopping up spills and wiping brushes, and is also used in the steaming process. If you prefer not to use pins on your silk, or if your frame is narrow, use **masking tape** as an alternative to pinning, and to fix silk or designs to the work surface. Small tabs are better than long strips as it is easier to adjust them if you need to reposition the silk. For cutting out your cards a **cutting mat** with a self-healing surface is best. You will need a **rule** to measure cards and draw straight lines and a **3B pencil** to trace designs on the silk. Designs which are to be mounted on coloured card should be stuck to **white paper** first. Use **double-sided tape** to fix your template to the work surface and to hold the silk in place while the design is being traced. It is sticky on both sides and sometimes has a backing strip which is peeled back after positioning. A word of warning: the tape can be very fierce, so if you use it, only peel back the corners until you have positioned the card correctly, then strip off the backing while the card is in place. Special **foil adhesive** is used to bond metallic foils to fabrics, and is usually available with the foil. A **hair dryer** can be used to speed up the drying process. You will need sharp **scissors** for cutting out and an **eraser** to remove pencil lines. To make a neat fold, score across the card with the back of a scissor blade. Use a **craft knife** to cut out cards and to sharpen pencils. **Aluminium foil** is used to cover the rolled-up silk during the steaming process. A **metal rule** is best when cutting card. If you want to make your own templates, use a **black felt-tip pen** to draw it out so it shows through the silk.

A selection of purchased card mounts and metal foils

Butterfly

This project is a good one to start with, as you only need three colours of paint and you do not even need a frame. It uses a very simple technique: the silk is folded before applying the colours so a symmetrical pattern is created when it is unfolded. The colours run along the creases, resembling the veins in a butterfly's wing.

The painted silk can be stuck on to a pre-cut shaped card, as shown in the project, and the surplus silk trimmed off. Alternatively, you can stick the painted silk on to an oblong of white card, then trace the butterfly shape given below on the back of the card. If you do this, the folded card and the silk can both be cut out at the same time, using a sharp craft knife or scissors.

If you use steam-fix silk dyes, follow the fixing method shown on page 9.

You will need

Butterfly-shaped card or white card plus template

Piece of Habotai silk slightly larger than the template

Polythene sheet

Craft knife

Scissors

Silk colours: I used golden yellow, magenta and ultramarine blue, plus violet mixed from magenta and ultramarine blue

Brush No. 6

Iron and ironing board or pad

Two small coins or weights

Spray adhesive

Full-size template

1. Protect your work surface with polythene. Cut a piece of silk a little larger than the template. The silk should be placed with the right (slightly shinier) side upwards.

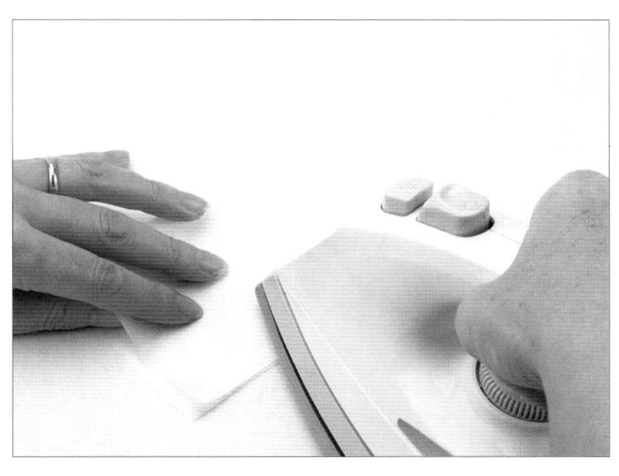

2. Switch on the iron. Place your work right side down on a pad of cotton material or an ironing board. Pick up the nearest corners and fold the silk upwards. Press in the crease.

3. Fold the crease you have just ironed in upwards so the silk is folded into quarters. Press in the crease again.

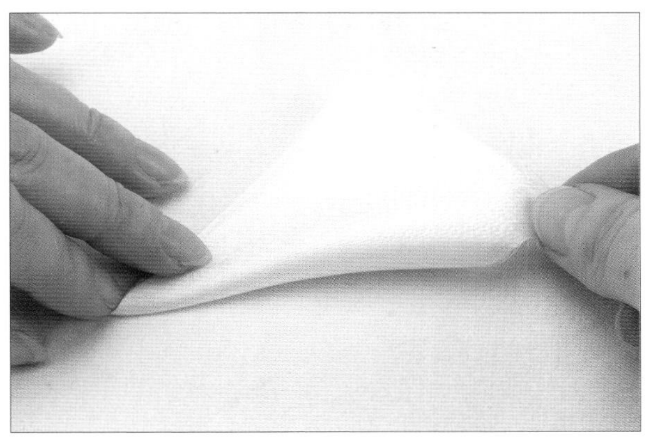

4. Repeat the process, folding the silk upwards and into eighths to make a narrow triangle. Press in the crease again.

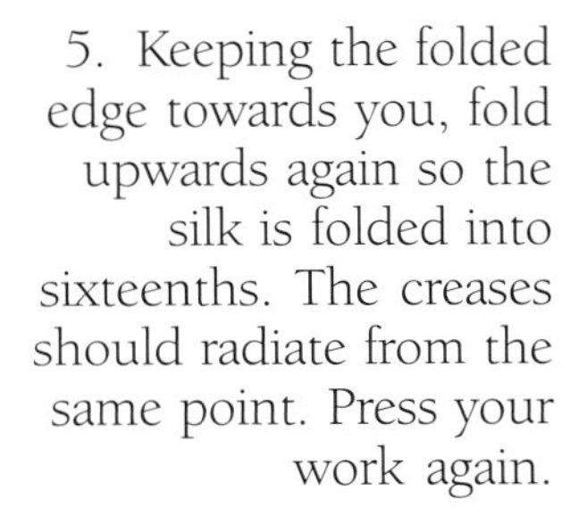

5. Keeping the folded edge towards you, fold upwards again so the silk is folded into sixteenths. The creases should radiate from the same point. Press your work again.

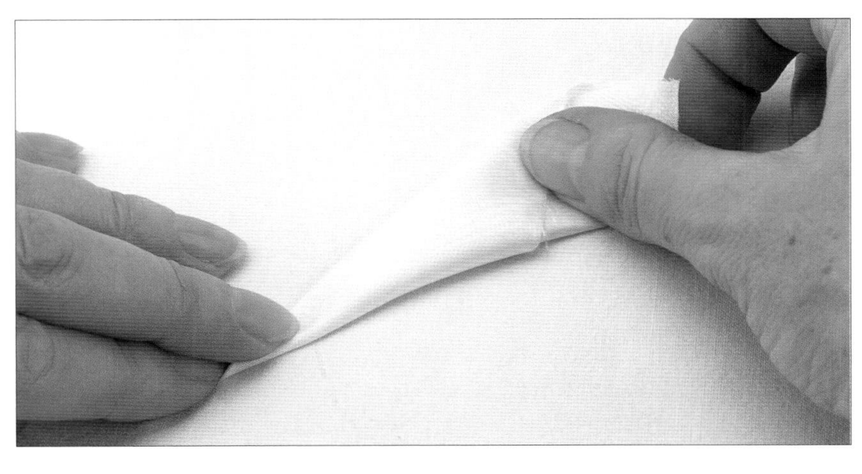

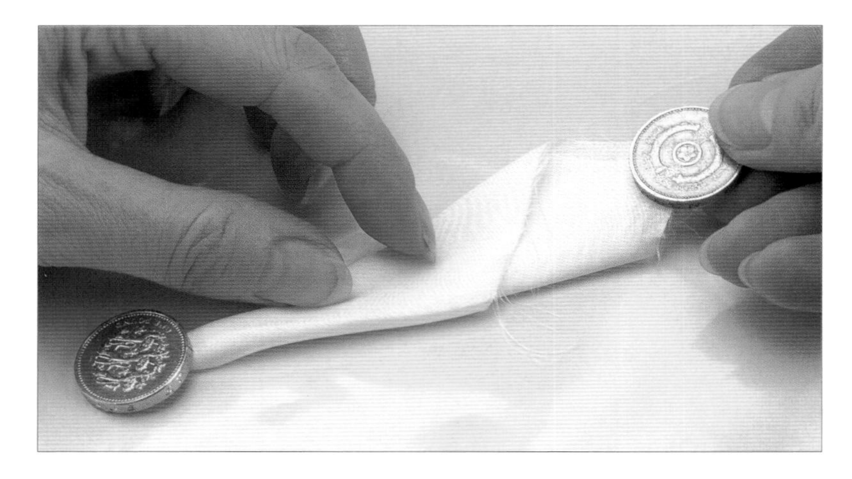

6. Protect your work surface with the polythene sheet and transfer the folded cone of silk to it carefully. Weight the ends so it does not unfold. Coins are ideal for this.

7. Using a dropper, drop the colours you plan to use into individual palettes, mixing colours and diluting them if necessary. Test the colours on a piece of scrap silk – see page 8.

8. With a No. 6 brush and beginning with yellow, apply colour generously to the end of the cone. Use a dabbing motion to ensure that it penetrates the layers of silk.

9. Make sure the yellow has spread under the coin, right to the point. Rinse the brush and dry it on absorbent paper. Working quickly and dabbing as before, add magenta next to the yellow, overlapping the edges of the yellow a little.

10. Repeat with blue, then finish with violet.

11. Use the end of a clean brush to lift the silk carefully. Check that the colours have penetrated the silk and apply more if necessary. Leave your work to dry folded.

12. Unfold the silk and iron it flat. This will fix iron-fix paints. If you have used steam-fix dyes you should fix them at this point, using the method shown on page 9.

13. Protect your work surface with paper. Lay the silk on the paper with the right side down and spray it lightly and evenly with adhesive. Position the card template carefully on the back of the painted silk, so that the centre of the butterfly's body aligns with its centre fold.

14. Turn the silk over and smooth out any air bubbles or creases with your fingertips. Leave it to dry for a few minutes.

15. Cut carefully round the template. The spray adhesive will stop the silk fraying.

Opposite: a collection of butterflies ready to take flight

Below: the finished card

Bright Angles

These jolly little squares are painted using black outliner to contain the separate colours. This project also introduces simple colour mixing, using red, yellow and two blues to make orange, green and a range of violets. Part of the fun and the skill of silk painting is the colour mixing. Practise it as much as you can, as it will save you from having to buy lots of ready mixed colours.

In this project, the silk is stuck into a three-fold aperture mount, which gives it a very neat finish. You may find that it is easier to position your silk in the aperture by spray mounting it on to paper first, as in the Peony project on page 24. Another effective way of using an aperture card mount is to cut a small square of polyester wadding, slightly smaller than the aperture, and spray mount it under the silk so the silk is slightly padded.

You will need

Square of Habotai silk, torn carefully along the grain

Double-sided adhesive tape

Rule

Scissors

3B pencil

Silk pins

Frame

Black outliner

Silk colours: I used golden yellow; orange made from red and golden yellow; red; green made from yellow and cyan; ultramarine blue; cyan, and a range of blues and violets made from different proportions and concentrations of red and ultramarine blue

Brush No. 6

Three-fold square white aperture card

Spray adhesive

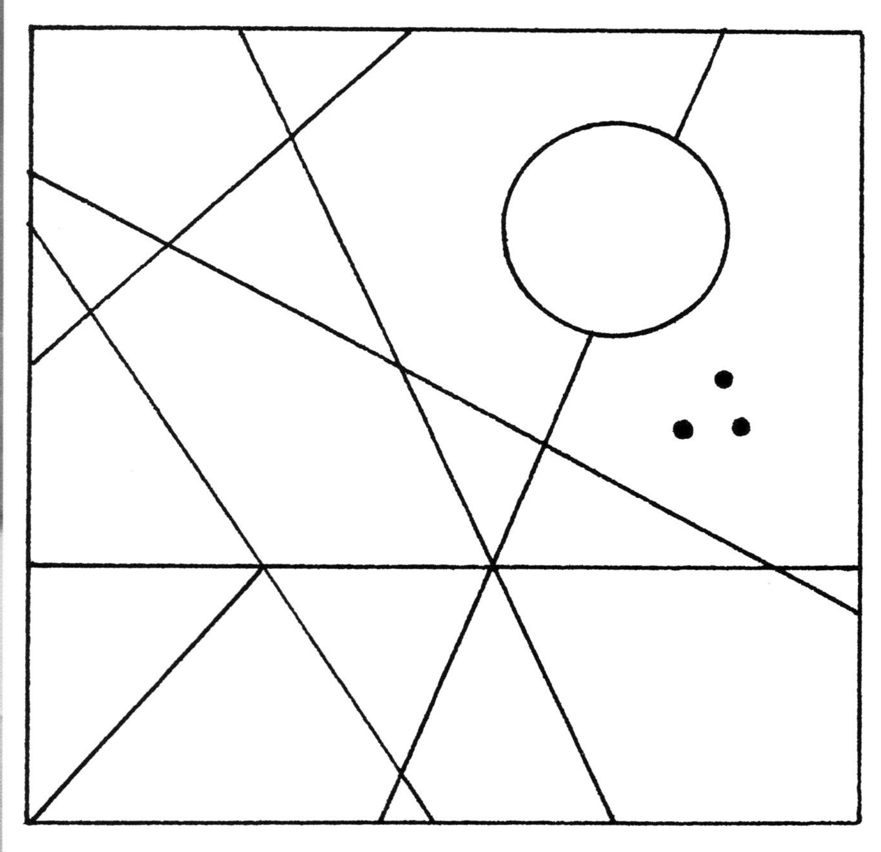

Full-size template

Tip

Some black outliners are rather thick and sticky and seem to smudge even after they have been fixed. Experiment with different makes until you find one you like.

Practise applying outliner on a spare piece of silk first. Follow the pencil lines as closely as possible but do not worry if they are a bit wavy – just make this part of your design. Make sure there are no gaps, particularly where lines join.

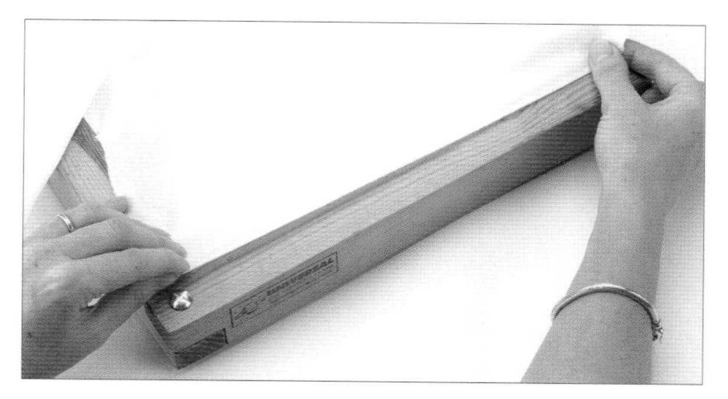

1. Measure the silk against the frame.

2. Leaving extra for pinning, nick the silk with scissors.

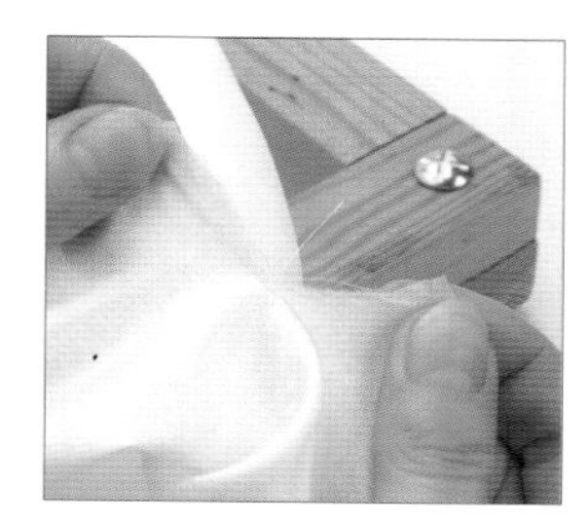

3. Tear firmly, then repeat the process on the other edge.

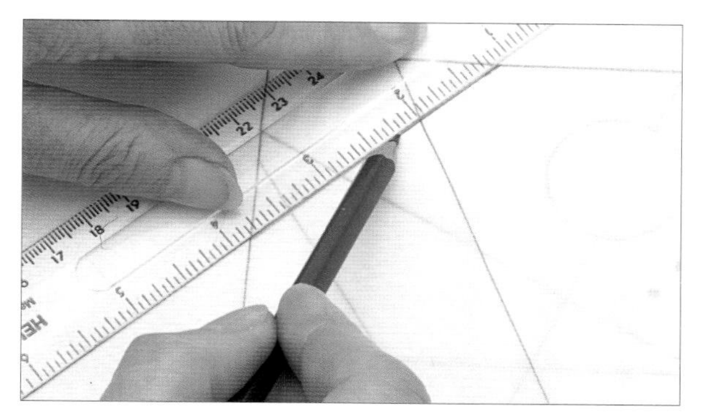

4. Use double-sided tape to fix the template and silk to the work surface. Position the silk on the design, making sure it is square to the edges, and smooth down on the tape. Draw in the straight lines lightly using a rule.

5. Draw in the circle using a small circular object such as a coin or bottle top.

6. Remove the template. Pin the silk to the frame so it is smooth and taut, spacing the pins evenly about 5cm (2in) apart, or use masking tape.

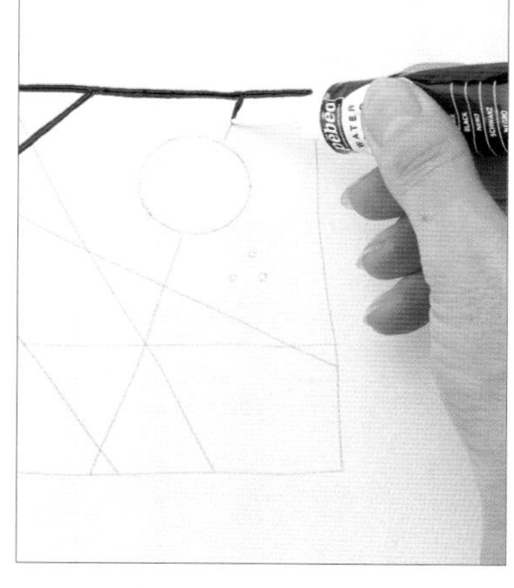

7. Outline the design using the black outliner, holding it at an angle of about 45° and pressing the spout against the silk. Leave to dry.

8. Mix the colours you plan to use and test them on a piece of silk (see page 8). Paint in the orange circle.

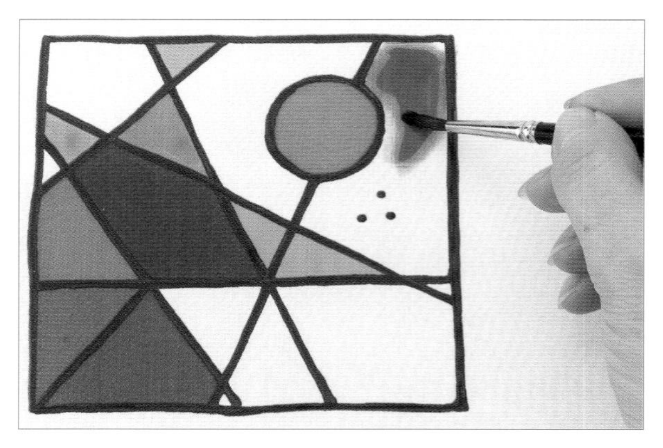

9. Paint in sections of the design, allowing the colours to spread up to the outlines. Dab your brush dry every time you change colour.

10. Complete the design, using either the colours shown or your own choice. Allow to dry, then fix the colours (see page 9).

11. Protect your work surface with scrap paper or polythene and protect the right-hand flap of the card with paper. Spray adhesive lightly across the aperture and left-hand fold.

12. Place the silk carefully in the card, making sure it is in the correct position and that the silk is the right way up when viewed through the aperture. Smooth down.

13. Fold in the left-hand flap over the aperture, enclosing the silk, and smooth down the edge of the aperture with your fingertips. Note that the adhesive remains workable for some time, so you can peel off the silk and reposition it if necessary.

The finished card

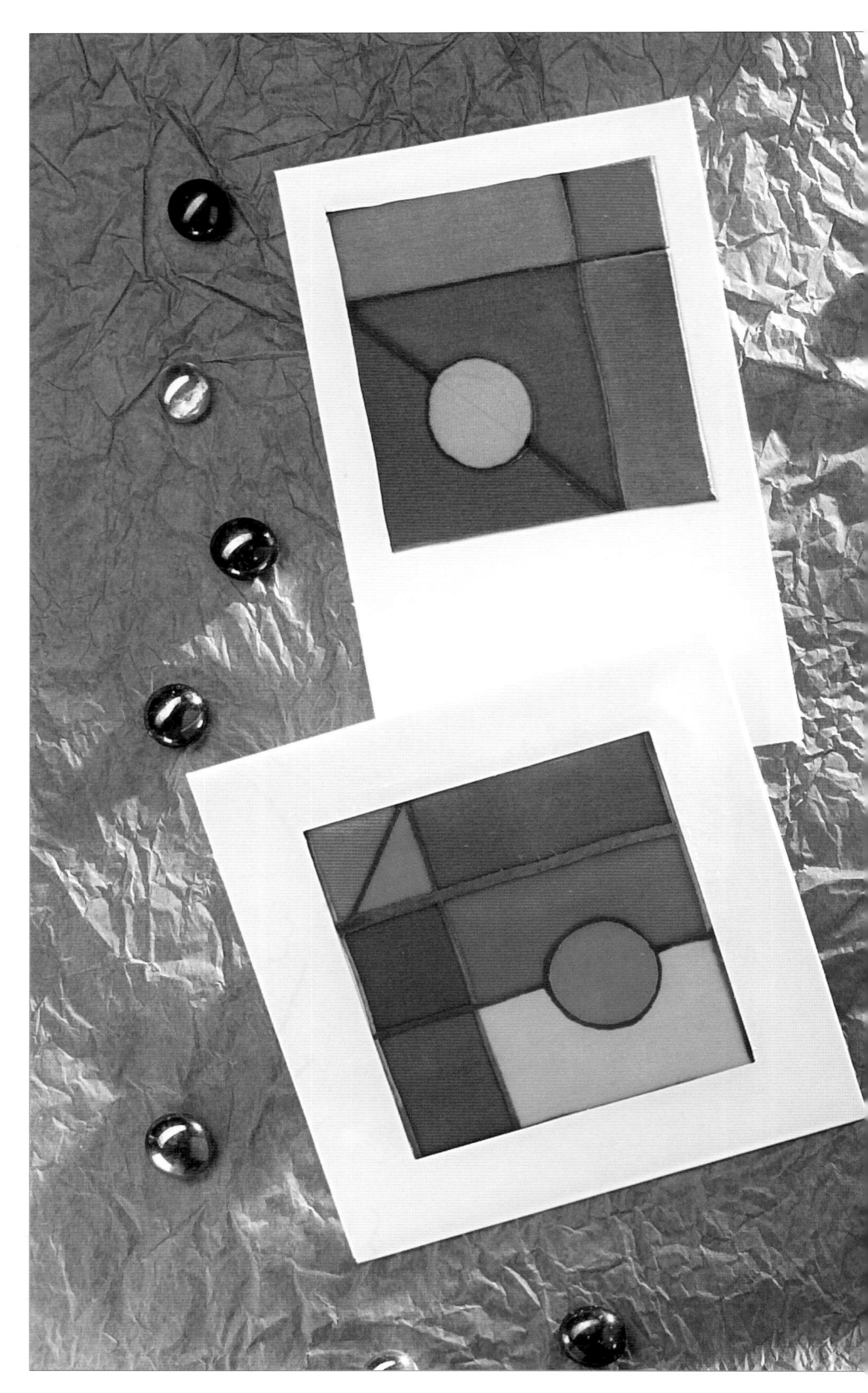

Bright Angles
Variations on a similar geometric theme, shown with aperture mounts and also raised mounts *(see page 38 for method)*

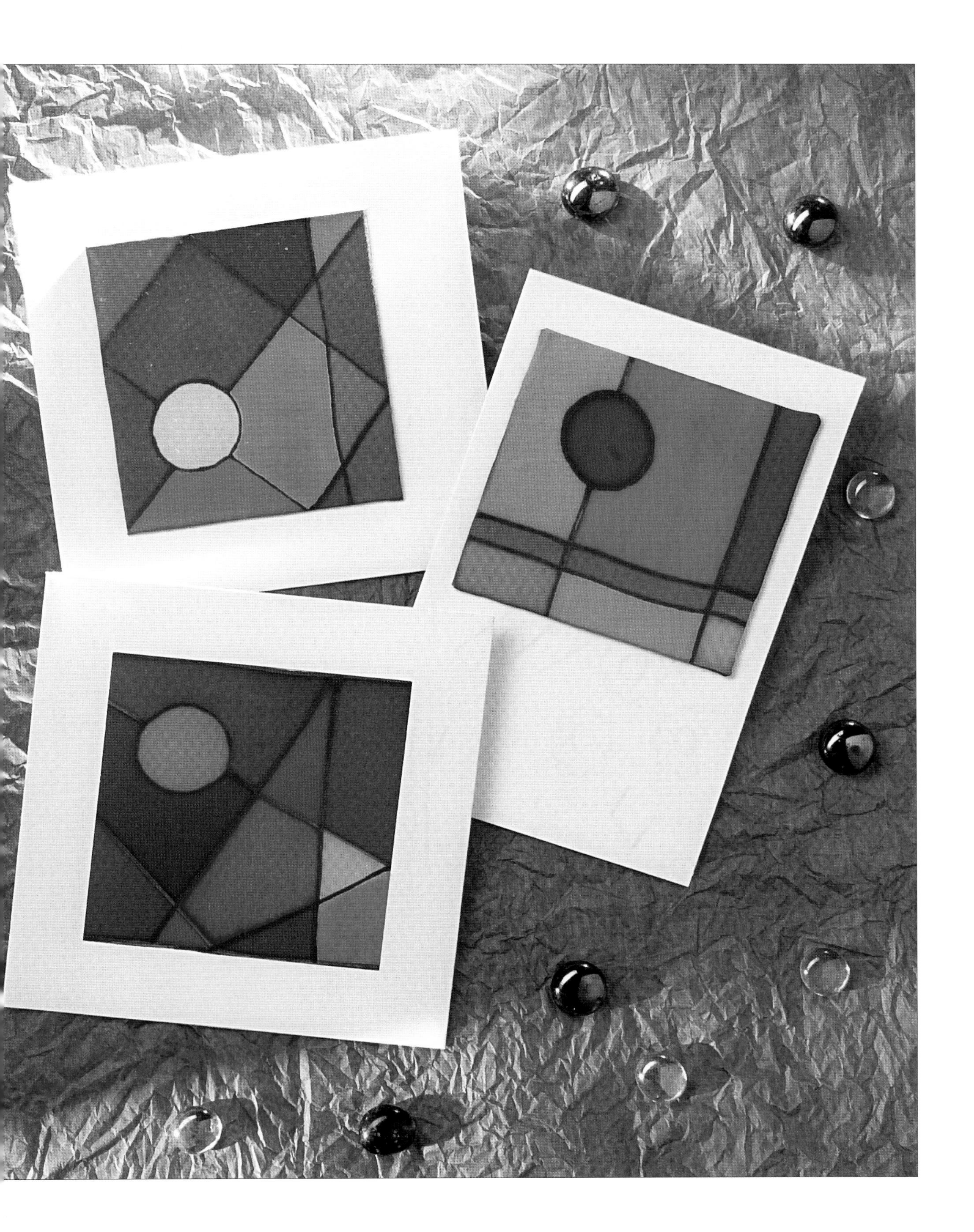

Peony

This peony is painted using a wet-in-wet technique, with bright colours that blend and merge to create a rainbow! The flower is outlined with clear gutta, which contains the colours and stops the silk fraying round the cut edge. Colours spread faster and more freely on dry silk, so the petals are dampened before applying the colours so they do not spread as quickly, giving you time to add extra colours to the white spaces. The colours blend as they dry, but you can halt the process by drying gently with a hair dryer.

If you use water-based gutta, try not to paint over the lines as it tends to stain them. You can remove water-based gutta by rinsing the silk after fixing, then ironing it to remove creases. Spirit-based gutta can be left in the silk, or it can be removed by rinsing with white spirit after fixing, then washing the silk in warm, soapy water to remove the spirit.

The painted silk is stuck on to a white paper base, which makes it easier to cut out the flower shape and does not affect the colours of the painted silk. The paper-backed silk can then be stuck on to coloured card if you wish.

You will need

Piece of Habotai silk large enough to pin to a frame

3B pencil

Frame

Scissors

Silk pins

Double-sided tape

Clear outliner (gutta) and a small plastic bottle with a No. 6 nib, *or* a tube of clear gutta

Silk colours: I used golden yellow; magenta; cyan; ultramarine; violet made from ultramarine and magenta, and green made from golden yellow and cyan.

Brush No. 6

White backing paper

Two-fold square card mount

Spray adhesive

Full-size template

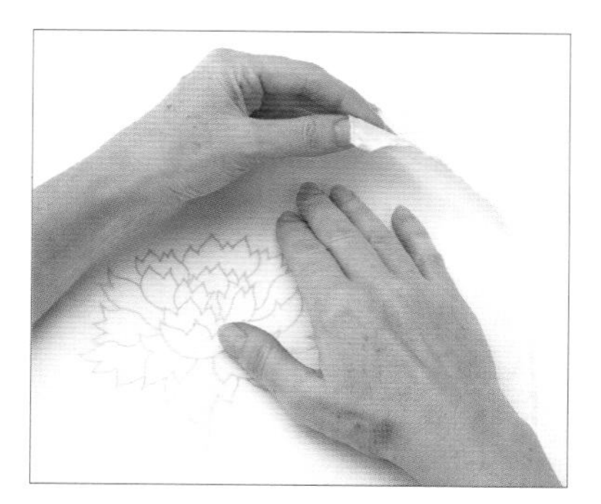

1. Attach the template and silk to your work surface with double-sided tape.

2. Transfer the outlines of the design very lightly to your silk using a 3B pencil.

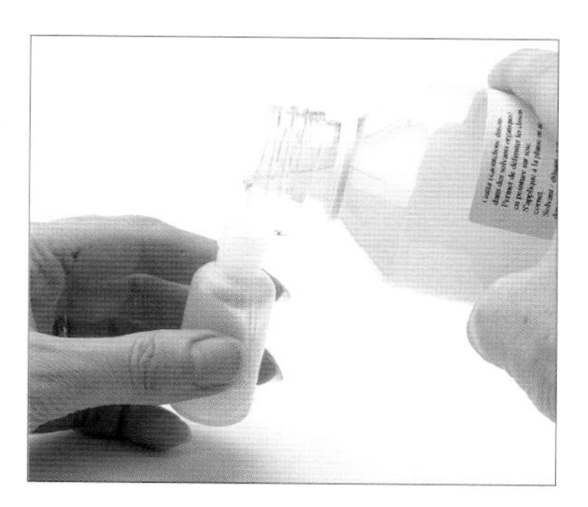

3. Pour clear gutta into a bottle and fit with a gutta nib, or use a tube of gutta.

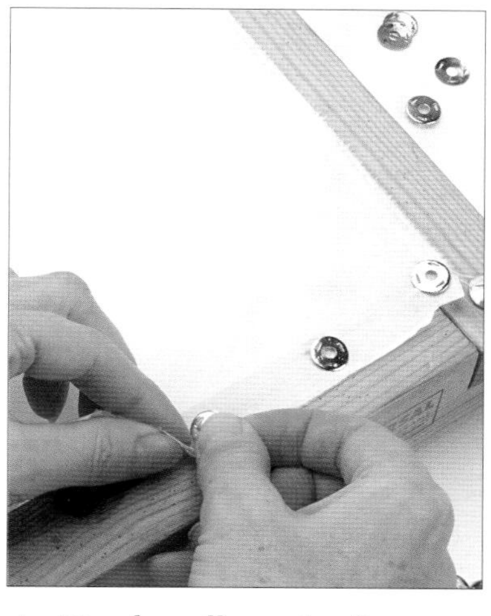

4. Pin the silk to the frame (see page 19).

5. Outline carefully over the pencil lines, holding the bottle at a 45° angle and pressing the nib on to the silk. Make sure the lines join without any gaps. Set aside to dry or use a hair dryer.

Tip

To check that there are no gaps in the gutta outline before you start to paint the silk, hold your work up to the light and any breaks in the line will be easy to spot.

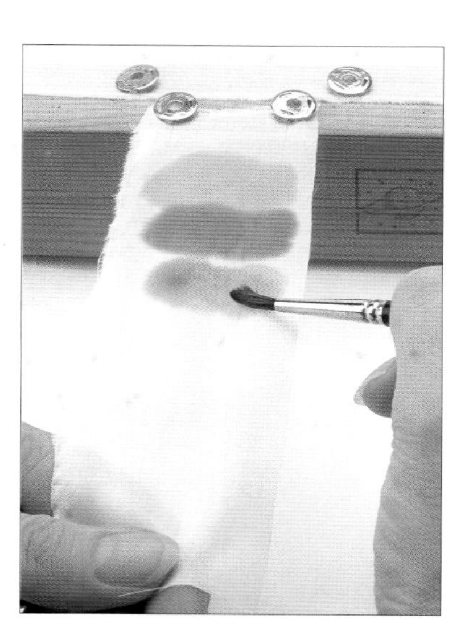

6. Mix your colours and test them on a spare piece of silk, diluting with water or diffusing medium.

7. Paint the petals with a little plain water to dampen the silk.

8. Working quickly, touch some yellow into a few of the flower petals.

9. Add cyan immediately and let the colours blend on the damp silk to create green.

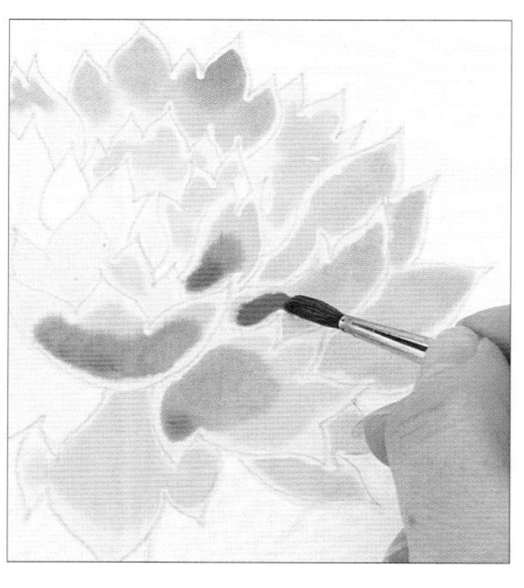

10. Add magenta into some petals, letting the colours mingle on the damp silk.

11. Add more touches of cyan, then some violet, to the petals towards the left to create a cooler, shadowed effect.

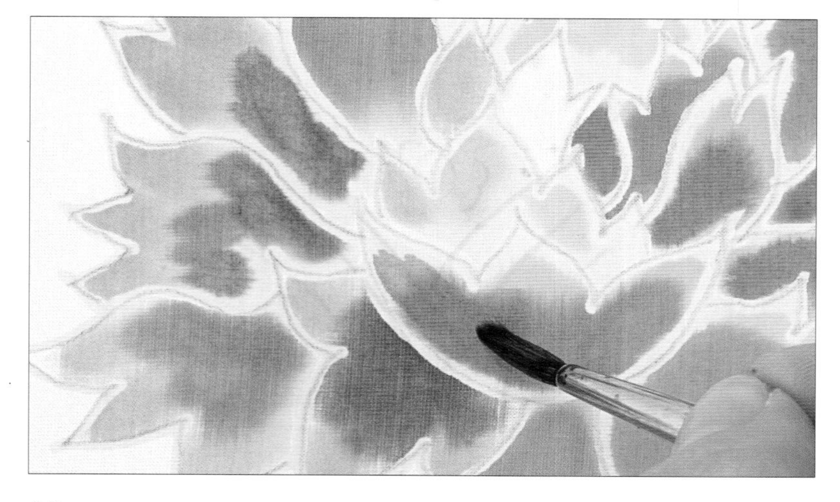

12. Keep adding colours until all the spaces have been filled.

13. Complete the flower by blending the colours in places with the tip of the brush, until you are satisfied with the effect.

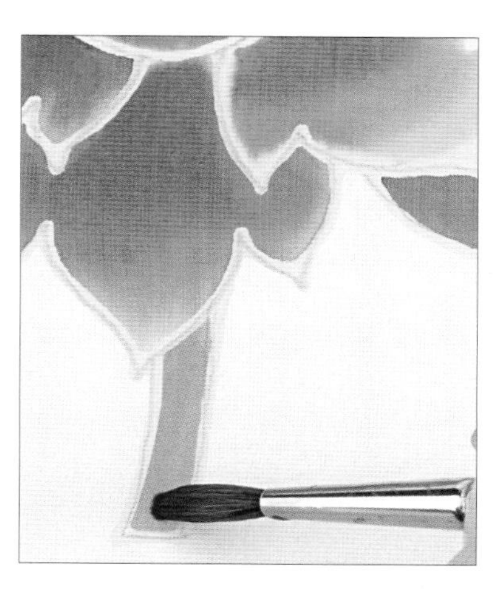

14. Paint the stalk green. Leave to dry, then remove from the frame and fix.

15. Iron the silk to remove any creases. Cover the reverse of the design evenly with spray adhesive.

16. Mount the design on plain white paper.

17. Smooth the silk down with your fingertips. Leave it to dry for a few minutes.

18. Cut round the outside of the gutta lines with scissors.

19. Spray the paper-backed side of the design with adhesive. Position the design carefully in the centre of the card mount. Smooth down.

Opposite: a selection of peony cards showing designs outlined with silver, gold and bronze and the use of coloured card mounts.

Below: the finished card

Magic Carpet

This richly coloured silk card has a touch of Eastern promise, and is perfect for a festive greeting to a friend. The edges of the silk are fringed to make it look like a little carpet before you stick it to the card.

This project uses a glitter pen, which not only adds sparkle to your painted silk but also acts as a resist, preventing the colours spreading to adjoining areas. The silk is painted with blended colours and allowed to dry before applying the glitter, which is supported in a clear medium, so that it lies over coloured rather than white silk. Finally, sections of the work are over-painted using a darker shade, which changes the background subtly as it moves across them.

You will need

Piece of Habotai silk large enough to pin to a frame

3B pencil

Frame

Silk pins

Silk colours: I used golden yellow; magenta; ultramarine blue, and a violet shade mixed from ultramarine and magenta

Brushes Nos. 6 and 8

Glitter outliner

Two-fold oblong white watercolour card for mounting the silk

Spray adhesive

Scissors

Full-size template

Tip

You can make up your own designs by drawing with the glitter pens directly on to the dry, blended background. This spontaneous approach saves the time that is spent tracing on a design and outlining it carefully, and is very useful if you want to make a large batch of cards.

1. Pencil the design on to the silk fairly heavily, so it shows through the background colours. Pin to the frame and apply gutta to the outer edge only.

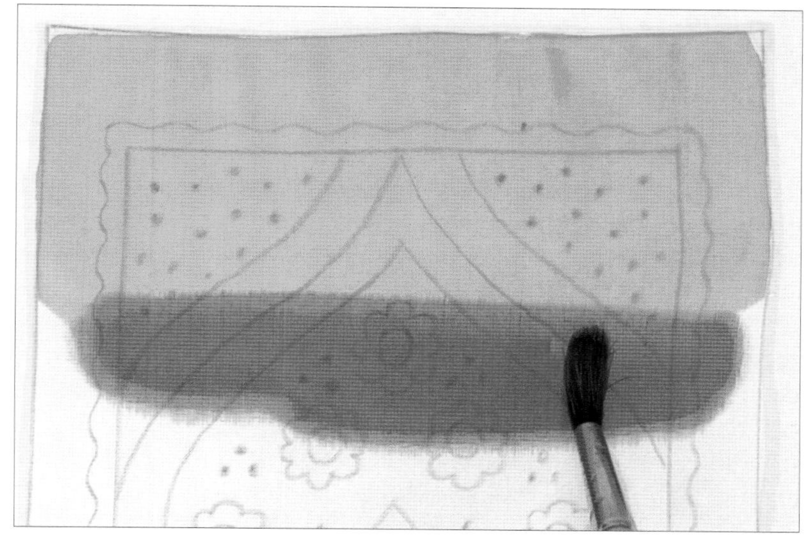

2. Allow the gutta to dry. Mix up the paints you will need. Using a No. 8 brush, sweep yellow paint across the fabric, followed at once by magenta.

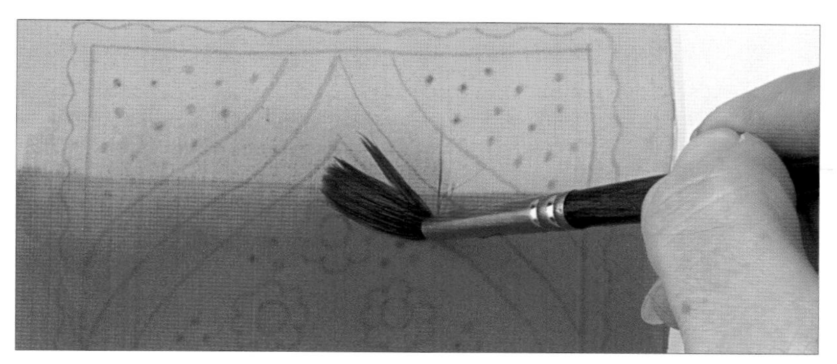

3. Rinse the brush, dab it dry and, working quickly, use it to blend the two colours briskly so there is no hard line.

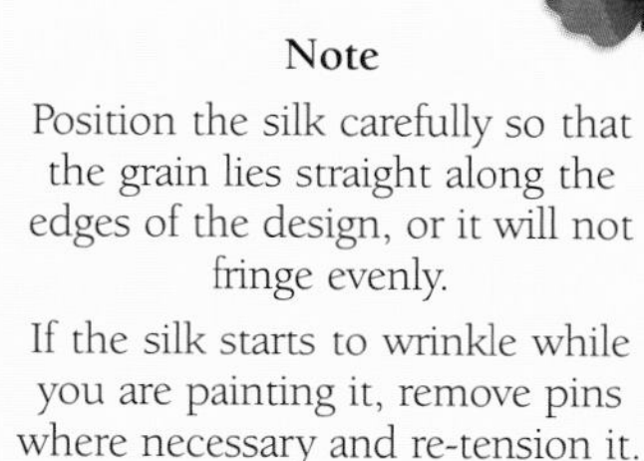

Note

Position the silk carefully so that the grain lies straight along the edges of the design, or it will not fringe evenly.

If the silk starts to wrinkle while you are painting it, remove pins where necessary and re-tension it.

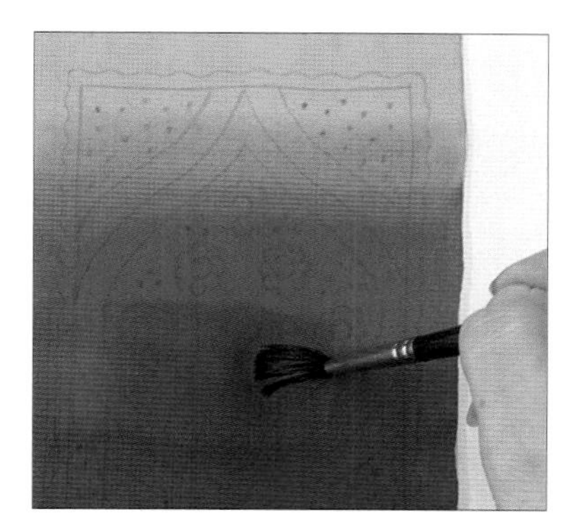

4. Quickly rinse the brush and apply violet, blending as before. Leave to dry.

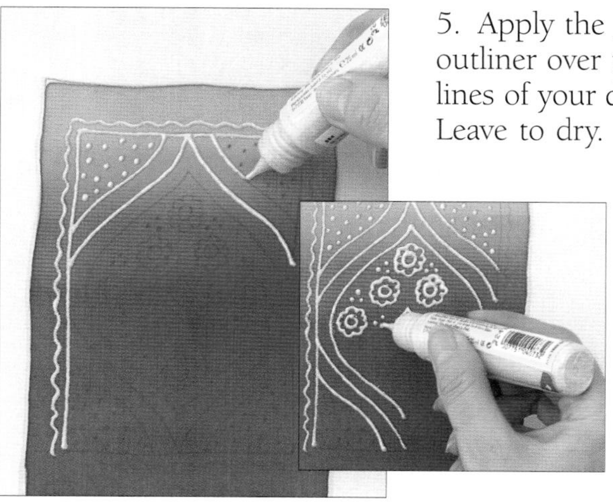

5. Apply the glitter outliner over the pencil lines of your design. Leave to dry.

6. Paint over sections of the design as shown (left and below) with ultramarine and a No. 6 brush. Touch paint into the chosen sections and between the dots, allowing it to spread to the outliner. Fix the silk (see page 9).

7. Trim the gutta edge from the silk using sharp scissors.

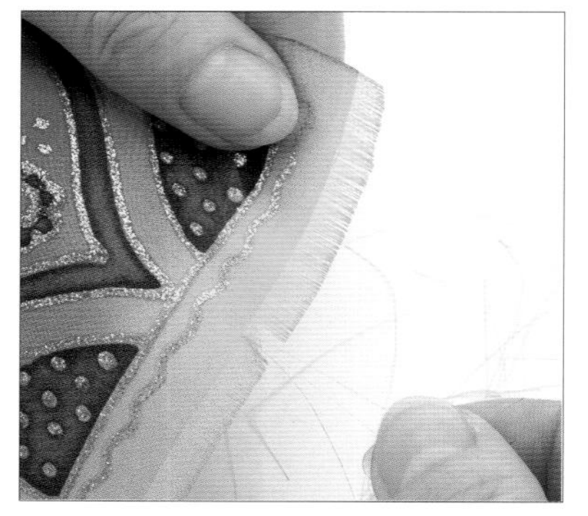

8. Pull out threads of the silk, a few at a time, to make a fringe at one end.

9. Repeat with the other end, making the fringes about 10mm (3/8 in) deep.

10. Mount the design on the card with spray adhesive, so there is a slightly deeper border of card at the bottom.

11. Smooth down the design, working from the middle outwards and stroking down the fringe with a fingertip.

Opposite: the finished card

Magic carpets
The number of possible variations is limited only by your imagination. This design lends itself perfectly to gift tags and bookmarks. The two cards at the bottom of the photograph show designs made with bold strokes of glitter paint, brushed freely on to the painted silk.

All That Glitters

You do not need to be good at drawing to make decorative card designs. This simple design with shiny lines and dots of gold foil is reminiscent of a seam of gold in a rock face. The wet-on-dry painting technique allows the colours to spread without restraint. Plain water applied in dots produces an interesting effect, but note that this works best when using steam-fix dyes. The raised mount makes the card especially attractive – for further examples see Bright Angles, page 18.

Metallic or holographic foils developed for textile and craft work are exciting when combined with silk painting, adding a mirror-like glitter that is especially effective on greetings cards. Patterns are drawn with flexible adhesive, which is usually available with the foil. The foil is pressed on to the adhesive and the backing is peeled away leaving the metallic or holographic coating stuck to the silk. Silk decorated in this way can be hand-washed, but do not iron directly over the foil.

In this project, the adhesive is simply applied in dots and lines, but it can also be sponged, stencilled or printed on. It should be applied fairly thickly, but make sure it is completely dry before laying on your foil or you will be left with a mess.

You might also like to try using the foil adhesive as a resist to hold back over-painted colours.

You will need

Frame

Silk pins

Piece of Habotai silk large enough to pin to a frame

Two-fold oblong coloured card mount

3B pencil

No. 6 brush

Mounting board cut a little smaller than the card

Silk colours: I used dyes in cyan; ultramarine; two shades of orange mixed using golden yellow and red; and two shades of ochre mixed using golden yellow, red and a touch of ultramarine.

Clear outliner (gutta)

Gold foil

Foil adhesive

Spray adhesive

Soft tissue

Hair dryer

1. Stretch the silk on the frame. Draw round the card mount with a 3B pencil.

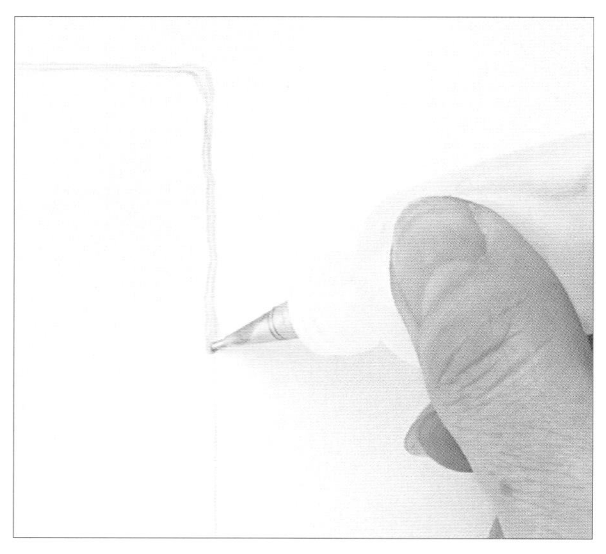

2. Apply clear outliner to the pencilled line to outline the edge of the design. Leave to dry.

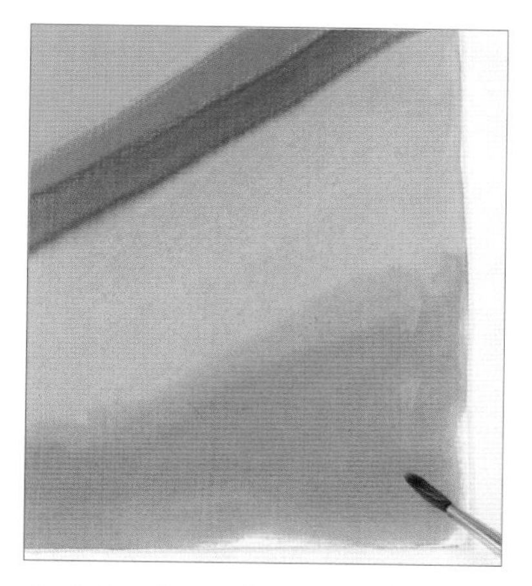

3. Mix the colours and paint diagonal stripes across the silk as shown. Leave to dry.

4. Over-paint part of the pale ochre section with a stripe of the deeper ochre.

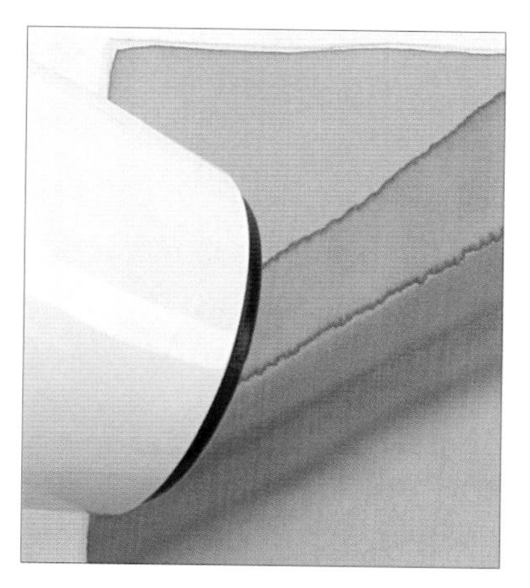

5. Wet colour spreads across dry, so control the spread of the stripe using a hair dryer.

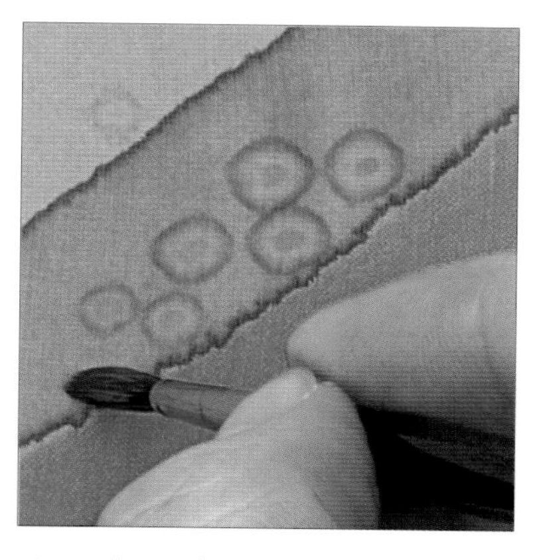

6. When the silk has dried completely, rinse your brush and touch its damp tip on to the silk to create spots.

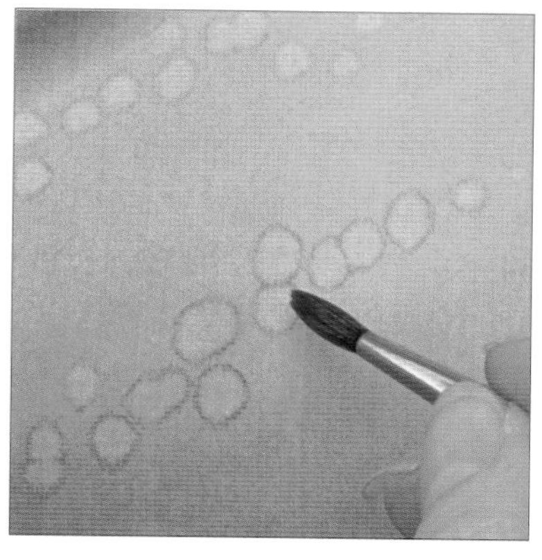

7. Paint more plain water dots on the orange section. You can stop them spreading too far by using a hair dryer.

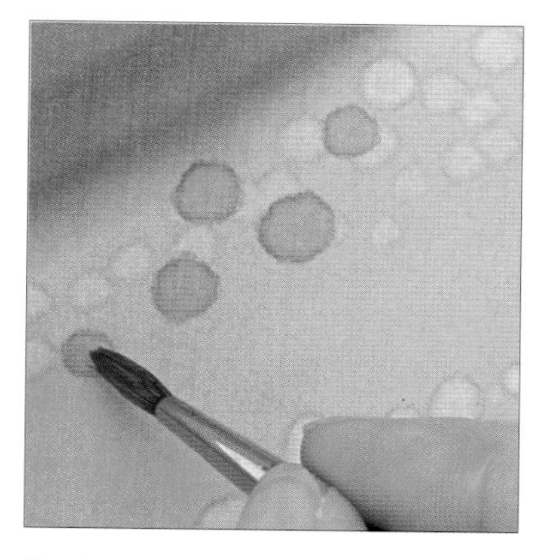

8. Use orange to paint in some darker dots to accent the design.

Tip

It is best to steam-fix the silk before applying the foil, because the foil adhesive can stick to the steaming paper or ironing cloth and make the foil crinkle. To apply the adhesive, you can lay the fixed silk on a sheet of polythene, or you may prefer to replace it on the frame. If you do this, smudges are less likely and the adhesive will dry more quickly. The silk should be unpinned and laid flat on your work surface to apply the foil.

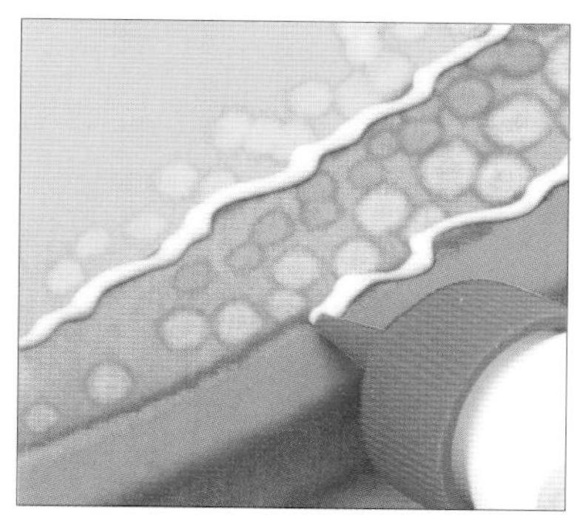

9. Apply wavy lines of foil adhesive to your design.

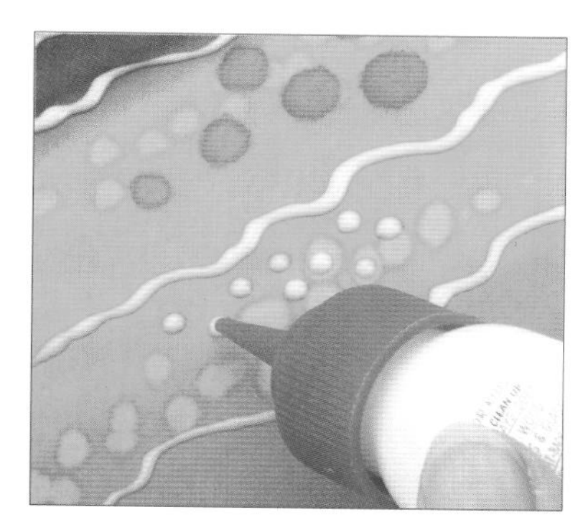

10. Add some dots of foil adhesive to selected areas. Leave until completely dry.

11. With the coloured, metallic side upwards, lay the foil over the adhesive.

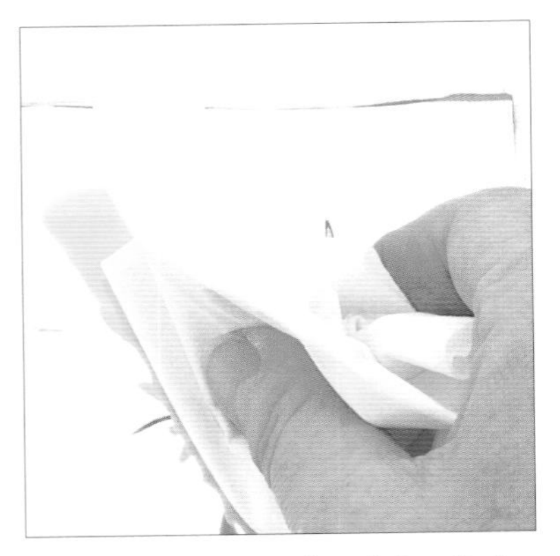

12. Rub the back of the foil gently with soft tissue to stick it to the adhesive.

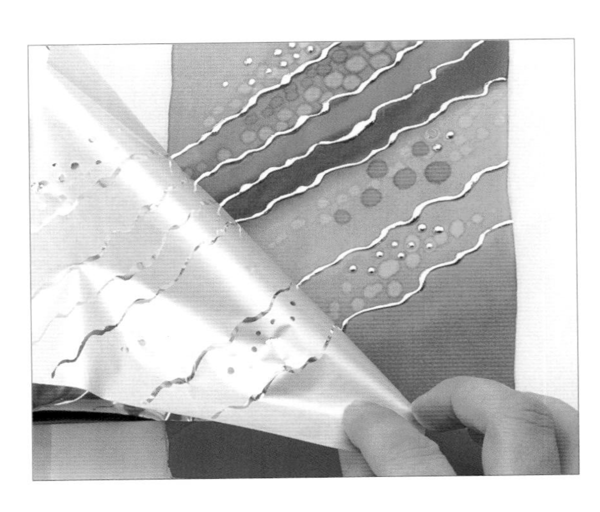

13. Peel off the foil carefully.

Tip

If the metal foil does not attach properly to any areas of adhesive, reapply it following steps 11-13

Making a raised mount

14. Trim the edges of the design, spray with adhesive and position on the mounting board.

15. Fold over and smooth down the two long edges.

16. Re-spray the corners. Fold and stick down the two shorter edges.

17. Re-spray the back of the mounted design and stick to the card, or use double-sided tape.

The finished card

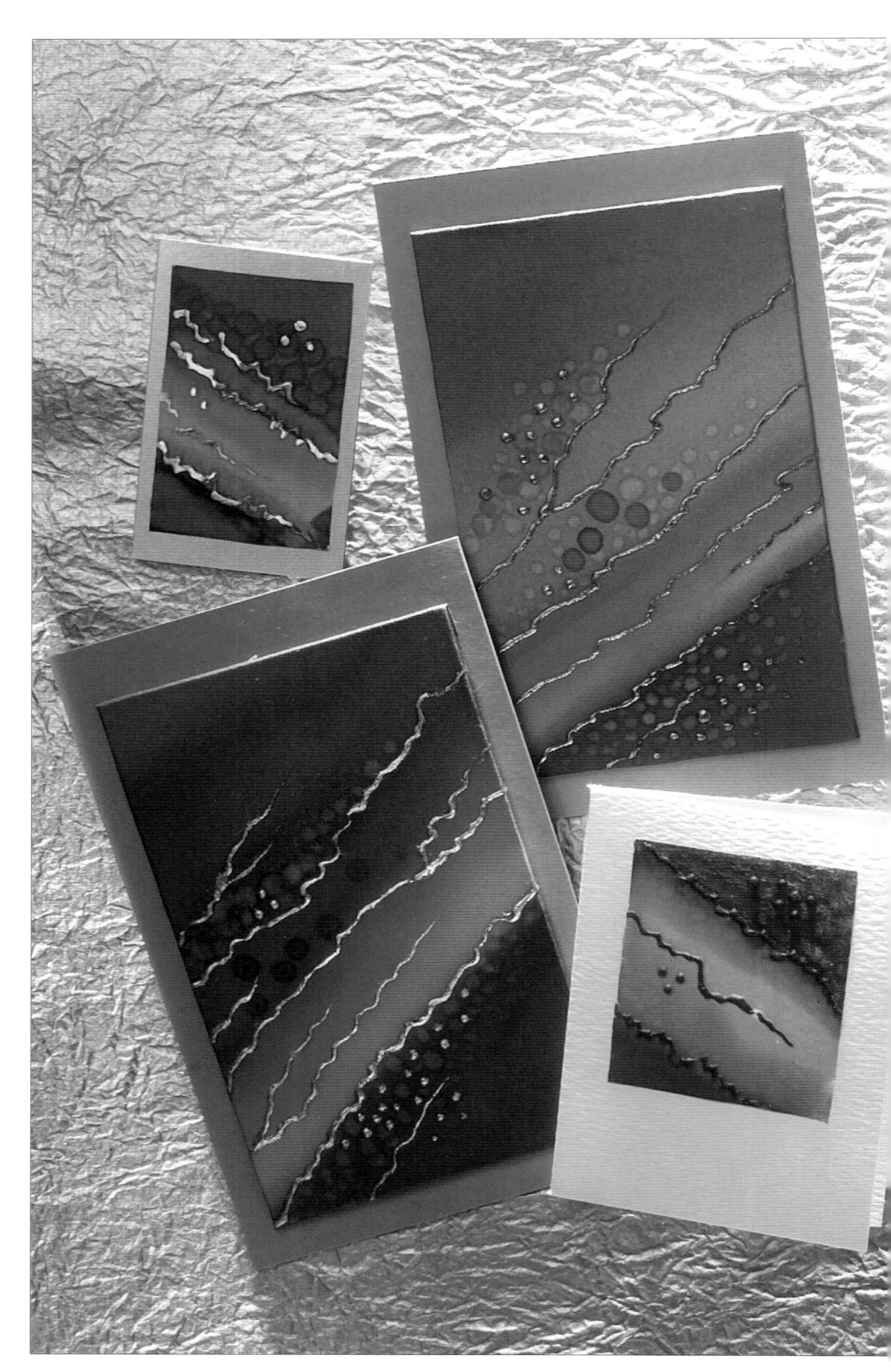

All That Glitters...
cards and gift tags in gold, silver, holographic and coloured foils, on raised mounts (see page 38 for method).

With Love

Paint a special card for someone you love. This project uses gold outliner as a resist and shows how to shade and blend the colours in the rose petals to create a three-dimensional effect. The metallic outliner prevents the silk from fraying, giving a neat edge to the design.

This design can be adapted for a wedding or birthday using silver or pearlised outliner and varying the colours, or make your own design by tracing a favourite flower from a plant catalogue or book. Designs can be enlarged on a photocopier.

You will need

Piece of Habotai silk large enough to pin to a frame

Frame

Silk pins

3B pencil

Brush No. 6

Gold outliner

Silk colours: I used red; the same red diluted with water or diffusing medium to make pink; three different shades of green mixed from lemon yellow and cyan; magenta, and mauve mixed from ultramarine and red.

Large two-fold white card mount

Spray adhesive

The template for the card (shown at 80° of full size – enlarge on a photocopier).

1. Trace the design lightly on the silk with a pencil. Attach to a frame. Outline carefully with gold, and leave to dry.

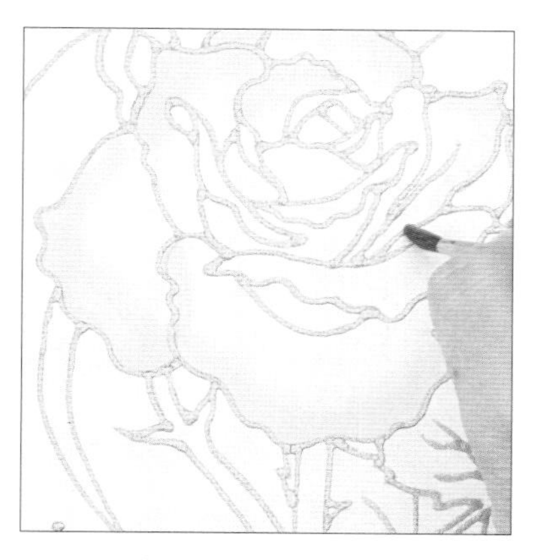

2. Apply plain water to the edges of the petals on the main rose, where you want the effect to be very pale.

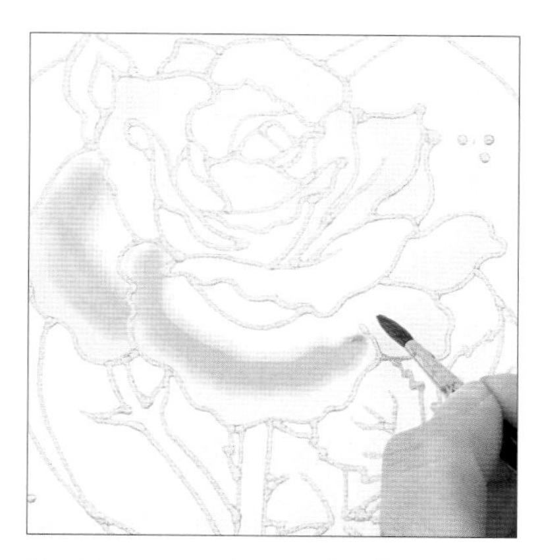

3. Paint in the pink shade next to the plain water so it begins to blend.

4. Working quickly, paint in the darker red next to the pink. Leave some of the frilly edges white.

5. Blend in more of the darker red to shade the petals further if necessary.

6. Touch in the centre of the rosebud. Blend the shades carefully with the tip of a clean, slightly damp brush.

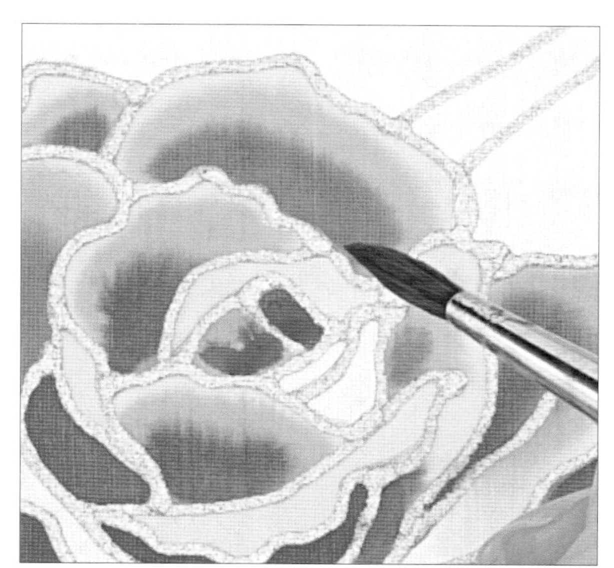

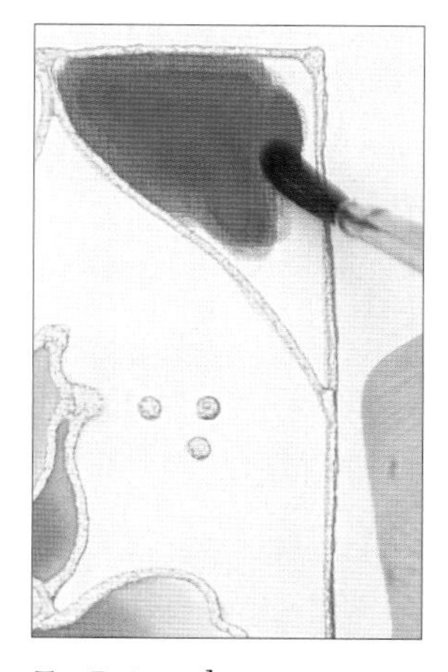

7. Paint the upper corners of the design with red.

8. Paint in the lower panels with red and the lower corners with magenta.

9. Use water to damp down the ribbon and heart shapes that will be painted wet-in-wet.

10. Paint in the ribbons and hearts using magenta, leaving white spaces for highlights. Paint in the light green sections of leaves, the stalk and the bud.

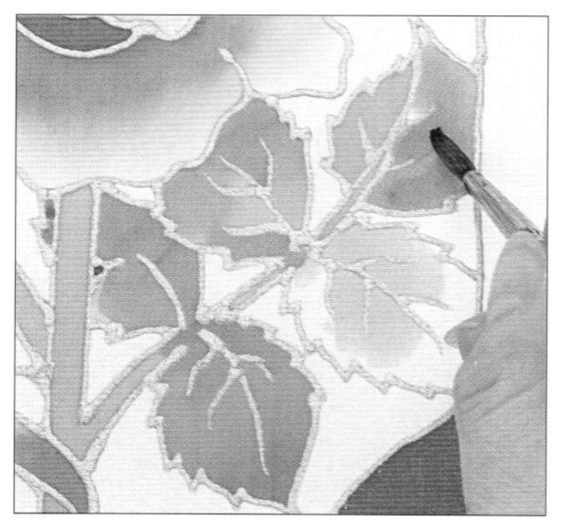

11. Paint the brighter green sections of the leaves.

12. Add brighter green accents to the stalk and bud.

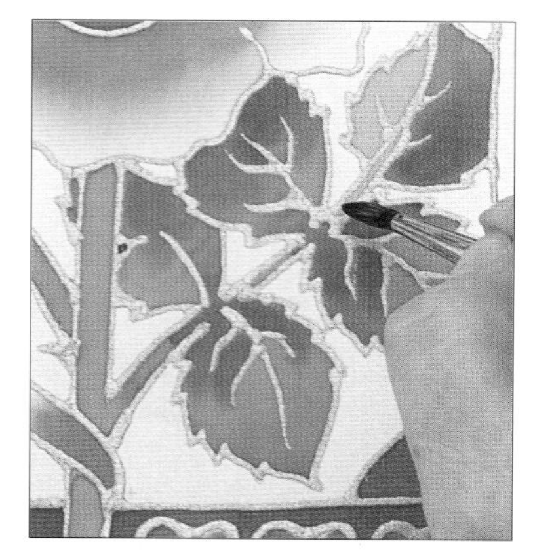

13. Put in the third green to shade the leaves.

14. Paint in the background. Leave to dry.

15. Fix the silk (see page 9) and iron. Cut round the outer edge of gold outliner to leave a fine gold border. Mount on to a large, two-fold white card using spray adhesive.

Below: the finished card

A bunch of roses

Varying the colours of the flowers and backgrounds can produce some very different effects.

Index

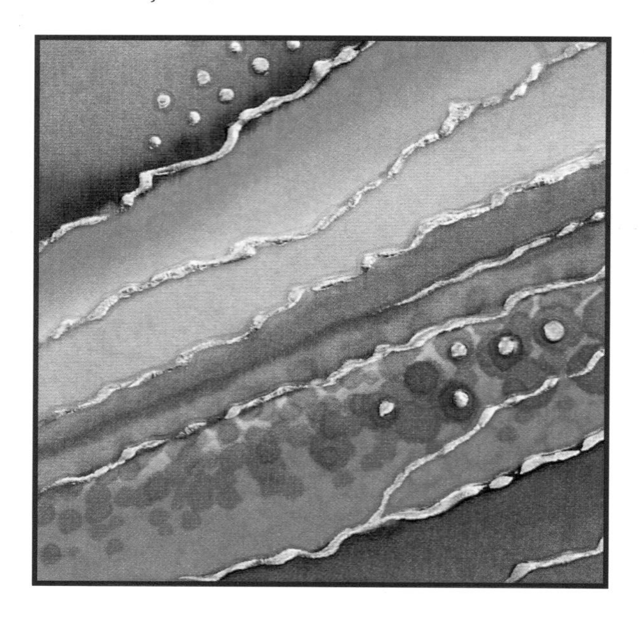